BOA
EDITIONS LTD

THE OASIS OF NOW

The Oasis of Now

Selected Poems of
Sohrab Sepehri

Translated from the Persian by
Kazim Ali
and Mohammad Jafar Mahallati

BOA Editions, Ltd. ⟶ Rochester, NY ⟵ 2013

First Edition

For information about permission to reuse any material from this book, please contact The Permissions Company at www.permissionscompany.com or e-mail permdude@eclipse.net.

Publications by BOA Editions, Ltd.—a not-for-profit corporation under section 501 (c) (3) of the United States Internal Revenue Code—are made possible with funds from a variety of sources, including public funds from the New York State Council on the Arts, a state agency; the Literature Program of the National Endowment for the Arts; the County of Monroe, NY; the Lannan Foundation for support of the Lannan Translations Selection Series; the Mary S. Mulligan Charitable Trust; the Rochester Area Community Foundation; the Arts & Cultural Council for Greater Rochester; the Steeple-Jack Fund; the Ames-Amzalak Memorial Trust in memory of Henry Ames, Semon Amzalak and Dan Amzalak; and contributions from many individuals nationwide.

Cover Design: Daphne Morrissey
Cover Art: Elisabeth King Durand
Interior Design and Composition: Richard Foerster
Manufacturing: Lightning Source
BOA Logo: Mirko

Library of Congress Cataloging-in-Publication Data

Sepehri, Sohrab.
The oasis of now : selected poems / by Sohrab Sepehri ; translated by Kazim Ali and Mohammad Jafar Mahallati. — First edition.
    pages cm
ISBN 978-1-938160-22-6 (pbk.) ISBN 978-1-938160-23-3 (Ebook)
Includes bibliographical references.
I. Ali, Kazim, 1971– translator. II. Mahallati, Mohammad Jafar, 1952– translator. III. Sepehri, Sohrab. Poems. Selections. IV. Sepehri, Sohrab. Poems. Selections. English. V. Title.
PK6561.S559A2 2013
891'.5513—dc23
                                2013013135

Lannan

BOA Editions, Ltd.
250 North Goodman Street, Suite 306
Rochester, NY 14607
www.boaeditions.org
A. Poulin, Jr., Founder (1938–1996)

Contents

3. The Traveler

Introduction

Sohrab Sepehri (1928–1980) was trained as a painter. He traveled frequently around the world, including to East Asia, Europe, and the United States. In 1964 and 1965 he took a long trip through China and Japan, learning about Buddhism while studying woodworking and painting. On his way back to Iran he stopped in India for several months. Upon his return home he wrote a rapturous poem called "Water's Footfall," a "lyric-epic" that shows marks of the influence of Islam and Sufi philosophy in addition to the Buddhist and Hindu philosophies and beliefs Sepehri was exposed to during his journey.

Sepehri is at home in the natural world, the phenomenological world that exists, and his God is neither bodiless nor remote, but incarnate in every piece of matter and as close as the nearest living thing. This experience of rapture floods the long prose lines of "Water's Footfall," which begins in a poetic autobiography recounting the death of the poet's father, his experiences dealing with grief and doubt, and then growing up and leaving home: "I saw a man down at heels / going door to door asking for canary songs, / I saw a street sweeper praying, pressing his forehead on a melon rind."

This conflation of ordinary things, discarded things, with the spiritual and divine seems to suffuse the poem. The small clay tablet upon which Shi'a Muslims press their foreheads when they pray is typically made, not of melon rind, but of sacred clay taken from the earth at Karbala, Iraq, the place at which Imam Hussain, grandson of Prophet Mohammed, was killed by his political rivals in the Damascus Caliphate. But here, the regular institutions of knowledge do not suffice. If Sepehri seems Sufi in inclination, it is the Sufism of Rabi'a, a faith of pure devotion that appeals—the institutions of learning and fixity and religious dogma the poet can do without:

> On the desperate scholar's bedside table a jug brimming over
>   with questions.
> I saw a mule bent under the burden of student essays.
> A camel slung with empty baskets of proverbs and axioms.
> A dervish stumbling under the weight of his *dhikr*.

Sepehri finished two other poetic works during the period following his travel—another long poem called "The Traveler," which uses a diary/dialogic form to explore some of the implications of the unsettlement that typically follows periods of spiritual wandering, and a set of highly charged lyrics called "A Measure of Green."

In the poems of "A Measure of Green" Sepehri combines autobiographical details, mystical ponderings and musical structures to create a style of poetry that was often criticized during his life and poetic career. Philosopher Soursh Dabbagh explains that Sepehri's "inclination toward more abstract thoughts subjected him to criticism by his contemporary literary critics such as Shamloo, Barahani, and Ashoori, who accused him of being disconnected from the social turbulences of 1970s in Iran."

Dabbagh goes on to explain that "Sepehri is far closer to the Heideggerian school of meditative thinking as opposed to Descartes' calculative thinking. He avoids the two modern philosophical approaches of knowing-that and knowing-how and prefers instead a non-theoretical approach that privileges a revelation of conditions of being, the same way that a dove understands water and wind."

Often in our translation process, we would have to pause over a verse or line or image and struggle to understand the multiple levels of personification and perception Sepehri was employing. In "The Fish Pass Along a Message," the fish in a garden pond liken the reflection of the sun on the pond (which has since evaporated) to a "fiery red carnation." When the wind blows across the pond's surface, the petals "crenellate" and the fish forget that the water would evaporate because of the hot day's "wily ways," though they also reason that the flower—the *reflection* of the flower in the water—was a "periscope" that allowed them (from beneath the water, naturally) to see the garden of Paradise.

Dabbagh explains, "Sepehri therefore enjoys a gnostic understanding of existence and finds himself in unity with the entire world. Like a gnostic seeker [he] desires to transform his whole existence into multiple eyes and maximize his non-intrusive observation of being."

We close our volume with the long poem "The Traveler." Here the lush density of "Water's Footfall" is replaced by sparseness; the pensive passion of the earlier poem gives way to a feeling of melancholy, a sharper sense of loneliness and emptiness; the melodic monologue of the earlier poem transforms to an introspective imagined dialogue. In all of his work Sepehri risks everything to place himself in the most vulnerable emotional positions that he can.

Many of Sepehri's deeply personal lyrics have become mottoes and slogans for individual freedoms espoused by younger Iranians, particularly those who became involved in the environmental movement and in the 2009 election protests. Just recently, when doing some research for this book, we found a line of Sepehri's used as a headline for an editorial in a Persian-language newspaper in Afghanistan that was criticizing religious fundamentalism.

Sepehri's abstract and meditative idiom, which made him subject to severe criticism of leftist political activists before and during the Iranian revolution, is relevant in Iran today exactly because his unconventional gnostic approach to language defies the official rhetoric of political religion. Ironically, he has gained far more relevance in current Iranian literature than some of the literature produced by his critics three decades ago.

Sepehri's verses are so commonly known in Iran that individual lines are often used by political thinkers to illustrate a point. For example, in a recent article entitled "Chastity or Head-Cover: which one is Unethical?" Soroush Dabbagh commented on an ongoing debate between Iranian ethicists and jurisprudents over dress code for women in Islam. To express his position that dress code is more a matter of Muslim history and jurisprudence rather than a moral act, Dabbagh resorted to the same Sepehri line that the Afghan paper used: "the haze of habit obstructs actual sight."

In these three powerful volumes by Sohrab Sepehri, we offer a haunting epic of the individual spirit's journey, informed by wild surrealism as well as a Sufi sensibility, extremely personal, highly charged—a smart and incisive yet tender examination of what is at stake for the individual in acts of travel and creation, both human and poetic.

Kazim Ali and Mohammad Jafar Mahallati
Oberlin, OH
November 2012

صدای پای آب

اهل كاشانم
روزگارم بد نيست.
تكه ناني دارم، خرده هوشي، سر سوزن ذوقي.
مادري دارم، بهتر از برگ درخت.
دوستاني، بهتر از آب روان.

و خدايي كه در اين نزديكي است:
لاي اين شب بوها، پاي آن كاج بلند.
روي آگاهي آب، روي قانون گياه.
من مسلمانم.
قبله ام يك گل سرخ.
جانمازم چشمه، مهرم نور.
دشت سجاده من.
من وضو با تپش پنجره ها مي گيرم.
در نمازم جريان دارد ماه، جريان دارد طيف.
سنگ از پشت نمازم پيداست:
همه ذرات نمازم متبلور شده است.
من نمازم را وقتي مي خوانم
كه اذانش را باد، گفته باد سر گلدسته سرو.
من نمازم را پي «تكبيره الاحرام» علف مي خوانم،
پي «قد قامت» موج.

كعبه ام بر لب آب،
كعبه ام زير اقاقي هاست.

Water's Footfall

I come from Kashan
and all is well.
I have a piece of bread, some smarts, a bit of wit.
I have a mother, better than the bright green leaf,
and my friends, like the river streaming.

I have a God as well who lives right around here somewhere…
among these night-blooms, or there at the foot of the white pine,
past the stream's consciousness, past all the laws and statutes of the
    reeds.

I am a Muslim:
The rose is my *qibla*.
The stream is my prayer-rug, the sunlight my clay tablet.
My mosque, the meadow.
I rinse my arms for prayers along with the thrum and pulse of
    windows.
Through my prayers streams the moon, the refracted light of the sun.
Through translucent chapters I look down at the stones in the stream-
    bed.

Every part of my prayer is clear straight through!

I begin my recitation
when I hear the wind's *azan* from the cypress tree minaret.
I start to whisper after the grass proclaims *allahu-akbar*,
    after the stream's surface sings *qad-qamat-as-salaat—*

My Ka'aba is there on the stream-bank,
in the shade of the acacia trees.
Like a light breeze, my Ka'aba drifts from orchard to orchard, town to
    town.

My black stone is sunlight in the flowers.

From Kashan I am,
a painter by trade.
Sometimes with paint and paper I build a cage of colors and offer it at
    market
to free your lonely heart
with the song of the poppy inside.

All these are dreams I know—
my canvas has no life, For example,
my painted pond is empty of fish.

From Kashan I came,
My ancestor was perhaps
a plant from India, or a clay shard from Sialk Mound,
or a prostitute in the streets of Bukhara.

My father died after the swallows' second migration, second snowfall,
second time sleeping on the roof-terrace.
My father died beyond time,
and the sky shone blue.
Then my mother shook herself awake, my sister's face flowered
and all the policemen became poets.
"How many pounds of melon do you want?" asked the merchant.
"How much will it cost to have a light heart again?" I asked in return.

My father, another painter,
was a lute-maker and played them too,
drew beautiful letters and words in ink.

Our garden stood on the shadowy slope of wisdom,
in the knot tied by the threads of thoughts and stems,
in the encroaching twist of gaze, cage, and mirror.
And maybe our garden was just a small arc of a grand green ecstatic
    spiral!
While sleeping there, I took bites from God's unripe apples,
drank long from the stream. I knew no philosophy, was ignorant of
    science.

As soon as I pulled the pomegranate apart
my hands were flooded by the dark-red fountain.
As soon as the lark sang, I leaned in to listen.
Sometimes the lonely lark pressed itself against the glass,
sometimes Longing turned up, throwing its arms around Feeling's
    neck.
Whimsy cut loose.
Life was a spring rain,
a sycamore inhabited by starlings,
Life was like a beam of light lying across a row of ceramic figurines,
an armful of freedom,
a pond filled with music.

Bit by bit the child crept away to the alley of dragonflies.
I packed up my suitcase, leaving the dream-village,
remembering with sadness blue and green dragonfly-wings.

I went to the banquet of the ordinary,
to the meadow of sorrow,
to the garden of mysticism,
the brightly lit room of science,
climbed up the stairs of faith.

I went to the end of the alley of doubt,
as far as the cool night air of contentment,
as far as the rain-damp evening of affection.

I went to meet someone at the far end of the alley of love.
I traveled as far as I could to meet another.
As far as the lamp,
the silence,
the fluttering sound of loneliness—

I saw many things on the way:
a child sniffing at the moon,
I saw a doorless cage,
inside a feathery light flapping its wings,

a ladder by which love might climb up onto the roof of the sky.
A woman pounded light with a mortar,
served for lunch bread and vegetables,
a plate full of dewdrops, a hot bowl of kindness.

I saw a man down at heels
going door to door asking for canary songs,
I saw a street sweeper praying, pressing his forehead on a melon rind.

I saw a lamb munching a paper kite,
a donkey assessing its alfalfa,
some cows dispensing sage advice.

I saw a lily addressed by a poet as "Your Honor..."

I saw a book with crystal words
written on pages made of spring.
A museum far from the gardens and trees,
a mosque far removed from any stream.
On the desperate scholar's bedside table a jug brimming over with
    questions.

I saw a mule bent under the burden of student essays.
A camel slung with empty baskets of proverbs and axioms.

A dervish stumbling under the weight of his mumbled *dhikr*.

The train sped by with its cargo of light.
With its cargo of theology, so heavy.
Its cargo of politics, so empty.
Its cargo of lotus seeds and canary songs.
A plane flew thirty thousand feet in the air
but reflected in its windows the earth:
        The crest of the hoopoe bird
        The calligraphed design on a butterfly's wings
        Reflection of a bullfrog on the surface of a pond
        The fly's flightpath through a lonely street

Reflected the sparrow's bright desire to swoop
from the sycamore's arms to the ground

The sun swells as it dawns,
the china figurine makes love to it all morning long.

Stairs lead down to lust's bed,
to the basement of wine and spirits,
to the laws governing the decay of roses,
to a mathematical understanding of the equation of life,
to terraces of revelation, lightning strikes of understanding.

Far below,
my mother was washing cups in the memory of the stream.

The town was visible,
a growing geometry of concrete, steel and stone.
Hundreds of city buses rumbling through with bare pigeon-free roofs.

The florist is having a fire-sale.
A poet hangs a hammock between two jasmine trees.
A schoolboy pelts stones at the wall.
A child spits apricot pits on his father's prayer rug,
a goat drinks long from a map of the Caspian.

A clothesline—bra flapping, impatient in the wind.

Cartwheel haranguing the horse to stop.
The horse wishing the driver to doze.
The driver longing for death.

Love we can see, waves,
snow, friendship,
words, even water,
the reflection of objects in water.
Cool shade of the body's blood-hot small cells,
the rain-wet alleys,

the eastern bank of sadness.
Season of roaming the alleyways looking for one another.
Sharp scent of solitude in the season's alleys.

A fan appeared fluttering in the hand of Summer.
Journey of seed to flower.
Journey of the ivy from one house to another.
The moon creeps under cover of night down into the pond's bed.
Rue splinters the meadow and spurts up from the earth.
Grapevines crawling down the wall.
Dew slicking the sleep-bridge.
Joy vaulting the moat of death,
all its catastrophes fading beyond words.

A crack in the wall fights off the persistent advances of the sunlight.
Stairs struggle against the Sun's long leg.
Loneliness fights the song.
Pears ache to fill the empty basket.
Pomegranate's jewel-seeds refuse to burst under the teeth's insistence.
Fascists march on the delicate touch-me-nots.
Parrot outdone by eloquence.
Forehead pushes itself against the cold clay prayer tablet.

Mosque tiles unpeel from the walls, flying toward defenseless
    worshipers.
Wind thrusts apart the rising soap bubbles.
Butterfly-army takes on the Pest Control Program.
Dragonfly-swarm versus Water Main Workers.
Regiments of calligraphy pens storm the printshop assaulting the
    leaden fonts.
Poetry clogs the throat of the poet.

Century undone by a poem.
Orchard beaten by a starling.
Alleyway conquered by two of us saying *salaam*.
Town defeated by a handful of wooden horsemen.
Every *eid* conquered by the troop of ceramic dolls.

A baby's rattle murdered on the mattress.
A story killed at the alley-opening of sleep.
Sorrow done in by song.
Moonlight shot at command of neon-lit night.
Willow tree strangled by order of the government.

Desperate poet executed by the snowdrop flower.

The whole surface of the earth was visible.
Order was on the march in the Ionian alleyways.
Owl's soft hoot in the Hanging Gardens of Babylon.
A cold wind blows scraggly bits of history east through the Khyber
    Pass.
A boat full of flowers floats on Lake Negeen.
In each crooked street of Varanasi, a bright lamp endlessly burns.

I saw the people,
their towns.
The mountains and meadows,
streams, the surface of the earth.
I saw the sprouts and plants growing through light and then darkness.
Animals in the night and then in day. Humans in darkness and in light.

From Kashan I am but
there I was not born.
I have no place of origin, no home.
With fevered devotion
I built a house on the far side of night.

In this house I live with the dark nameless grass.
I hear the breath of the garden.
Dark of night trickles down with the leaves.
Light coughs in the bushes.
I hear water wheezing through the cracks and crevasses.
Chirping swallows slip dripping down through the roof of Spring.
Sounds in the garden:
Solitude opens and closes windows noisily

Love roughly unjacketing, shedding its skin

Wings gather together to launch skyward
Sound of the soul splitting itself to the core
Desire's footsteps approach, lawful pulse of blood through the veins
In the water-well where the pigeons live, the pulse of dawn
Heartbeat of the evening that begins Sabbath
Sounds of carnations on the mind
Truth, like an unseen horse nickering
All forms of matter skitter like leaves across the ground
The sound of Belief's boots walking outside the window
Downpour kissing my eyelids wet with love
Over the sad tune of growing older
Over the sad song of pomegranate orchards
A window crashing down, its glass of happiness shattering in the night
Beauty's documents being torn to shreds
The wind like a bowl filling with loneliness and emptying itself and
    filling again…

I am close to the beginning of the earth.
I check the pulse of each flower.
I divine water's wet fate, the tree's green destiny.

My spirit flows in new directions, following all matter.
My youthful spirit
coughs out its longing.
Without other meaningful employment,
it spends its days counting raindrops that slowly mark the lines
of mortar between the bricks.
My soul is true as a rock in the road.

I have never seen two spruce trees at war.
Never seen the willow subletting its shade to the earth.
The elms offer their branches to the crows rent-free.

Wherever there is a leaf, I bloom.
The poppy rinses me clean in the bath of Being.

As can the wings of a housefly I also can measure dawn's weight.
Like a vase, I listen to the music of growing.
Like fruit in the basket I have a fever to ripen.
Like the tavern on the corner I stand on the border of languor.
Like the cabin in the dunes I fear eternity's tsunami.

Sun, richness, ever-yellow, join me, join me.

I want nothing more than an apple
and the scent of chamomile.
Nothing more than a mirror and my dear other.
I would never laugh at the child when his balloon bursts.
It doesn't bother me when philosophers split the moon in half.
I remember the fluttering of quail wings,
the color of the crane's long belly, the little goat's footprints.
I know where the rhubarb grows,
when starlings migrate, when partridges sing, to where falcons fly.
I know what the moon means, in the dream of the desert,
muttering in its sleep.
I understand the language of ripe berries bursting in the mouth of the
    climaxing lovers.

Life, that pleasant chore,
has wings and feathers wide as Death
and launches itself skyward searching for love.
Life should not be unmoving in our mind like a jar on the habit-shelf,
    just another little task on the list of things to do.

Life is like the hand that aches
to pluck June's not yet ripe figs.
Like a sycamore refracted in the fly's myriad eyes.
It is a bat flying in the dark,
the migrating bird's strange directional instinct.
Life is like a train blowing its whistle in the daydreams of the lonely
    tunnel-bridge.
Like from the airplane's windows it is a distant garden seen.
Newspaper coverage of a rocket launching spaceward.

An astronaut finally stepping down onto the lonely moon,
    smelling flowers of distant planets.

Life is like washing a dish.
Like finding silver coins shining in the gutter.

Life is like the square root of the mirror.
Flower raised to the power of eternity.
Earth multiplied by our heartbeats.
The simple geometry of breath.

Wherever I am, let me be there.
The sky is mine.
Window, mind, thought, air and love, this earth, this life are mine.

What does it matter
if loneliness sometimes encroaches, like a fungus,
growing thick in the dark?

I want to know:
Why is a horse noble and the dove beloved
but no one keeps a pet vulture in a gilded cage.
Why is the humble clover trodden upon rather than the red tulip.

I want to see anew and wash the words of the world
in wind and rain.

I close my umbrella
and walk in the rain.
Think and remember in the rain,
All the citizens of the town run out in the rain.
Meet friends in the rain.
Look for love in the rain.
Make love in the rain.
Play games in the rain.
Write, converse, plant lotus seeds in the rain.
Perpetually soaked, bathing in the pond of Everything-New.

Let's shuck our shirts and pants.
The forecast is rain.

Let's taste the sunlight, weigh the evening, the gazelle's light sleep.
Let's take measure of the crane's warm nest.
Let's not trample on the laws the grass has made,
let's drink wine instead
and open wide our mouths when the full moon rises.
Let's not dwell on the shadows of night
or think the earthworms are ignorant of the garden's deep world-views.

Fetch a basket:
fill it with all these reds and yellows and greens.

Let's eat bread and mallow flowers for breakfast.
Let's plant a sapling in the lilt and pitch of each word and line.
Let's sow silence between each syllable.

Ignore all the storm-free books,
the book in which the dew is not wet,
the book where the cells run together without membranes.
We don't want the fly to be buffeted by the hands of the wind.
We don't want the tiger to pass through Creation's door and disappear.
Without the worm, we would be hollow.
Repeal all the laws of trees if they deny the slithering caterpillar.
What would our clenching hands hold onto if there were no death?
Flight's logic crumbles if there is no light.
The sea stumbled about aimlessly until coral appeared in rocky blooms.

Don't ask where we are.
Smell the petunia instead, freshly planted in the hospital yard.

Don't ask where Fortune hides,
or why the heart's blood is blue or
what kind of night or breeze our ancestors felt on their skin.
Behind us, nothing alive.
Behind us, no birds' startling songs.

Behind us, no tempest, no wind.
Behind us, the spruce have shuttered their green windows.
Behind us, the spindles and spinning tops gather dust.
Behind us, all the wounds of history.
Behind us, the memory of a wave pours the rubble of stillness and
    emptiness ashore.

To the shore then,
to cast our nets upon the sea
and catch the freshness of water.

With a little pebble of sand
we can measure the weight of Being.

Don't curse the moon when you have fever.
(When I had fever, I noticed the moon come down
from the sky, my arms reached up.
Ever since I hear the goldfinch's song in my ears so much more clearly.

Sometimes my wounded feet
teach me the earth's changing terrain.
Sometimes in my sickbed, flowers multiply
and all the orange globes of lantern-light swell.)
Let's not be in dread of death.
(Death is not the end of the dove or the cricket.
Death constantly occupies the thoughts of the acacia trees.
Death dwells pleasant in the mind's meadows.
Death recounts the story of Dawn to the townsfolk at night.
Death slides inside my mouth when I eat the sunwarm grape.
Death quivers inside the robin's voice-box.
Death inked that calligraphy on the butterfly's wings.
Death sometimes harvests basil,
drinks vodka,
sits in the shade watching.
We all know:
Every deep breath is filled with the air of Death.)

Don't shut the door on fate; I hear it whispering from the hedges.

Pull the curtains open
and let the fresh air in.
Age and Growth can rest here
while all my little urges slip out into the garden to play,
doff their shoes and leap over the flowerbeds.

Let's let loneliness sing its song,
write a poem,
go out into the streets.

Let's forget about everything.
Forget everything when at the bank teller's window
    and when lounging under the sycamore.

Our mission is not to unpetal the rose's layered secret.
Maybe our mission is to float, drunk on the mystery of the rose.
Let's pitch our tents on the other side of the hill from Knowing.
Wash our hands in the leaf's green ecstasy and prepare the picnic.
Let's be reborn when the sun dawns.
Let's unleash everything,
water the flowers and rinse the windows,
    water and rinse our perceptions of space and sound and color.

Let's stitch Heaven between the two syllables of Being.
Fill and refill our lungs with eternity.
Unload the swallow of its burden of knowledge.
Let's strip all the names from the clouds,
from the sycamore, the mosquito, and the summer.
Let's climb up the wet blue rungs of rain higher and higher into Love.
Let's open all the doors to every being, to sunlight, to the green trees and
    gardens, to the dragonflies and cicadas and other winged creatures.

Maybe our mission
is to run between the lotus flower and the century,
hunting, hunting for an echo of truth—

واحهای در لحظه

به سراغ من اگر میآیید،
پشت هیچستانم.
پشت هیچستان جاییست.
پشت هیچستان رگهای هوا، پرقاصدهاییست.
که خبر میآرند، از گل واشدهٔ دورترین بوتهٔ خاک.
روی شنها هم، نقشهای سُمِ اسبان سواران ظریفیست که صبح
به سر تپهی معراج شقایق رَفتند.
پشت هیچستان، چتر خواهش باز است:
تا نسیمِ عطشی در بُنِ برگی بدود
زنگِ باران به صدا میآید.
آدم اینجا تنهاست.
و در این تنهایی، سایهی نارونی تا ابدیت جاریست.

به سراغ من اگر میآیید،
نرم و آهسته بیایید، مبادا که ترک بردارد
چینی نازک تنهایی من!

When Night Flooded Over

Full night,
a river flooding the banks of the spruce,
flowing off into the distance.

Moonlight paints the valley,
the mountain so silver-lit God had nowhere to hide.

We were there on the heights,
rinsed in light, completely unnoticed by Him.
The look we exchanged was clearer than it had ever been before.

Your hands like spring's first seedlings.
The terra-cotta wall between us slowly cracks
under the pressure of your exhale.

Our heartbeat thudded through the stone.
A classic vintage, the wine of summer flowed in our veins.
Moonlight enameled the sound of your slight shifting.

You were free, in love, in rapture. The soil and earth suit you perfectly.

All the bright green flooded the cool mountain air.

Shadows lengthened around us,
the pennyroyals dance in the wind.

All our ecstasies inseparable.

Light, Me, Flower, Water

No clouds, no wind—
I crouch at the edge of the garden fountain.
Fish swirling within—light, me, flower, water—
vines overhead with clusters of pure green life hanging down.

Mother is harvesting basil from the garden.
Bread, basil, feta.
Cloudless sky, dew-licked petunias.
Salvation is close by; it's right here in the midst of the flowers.

Light into the copper bowl sweet caresses pours down.
From the ladder leaning against the high garden wall, morning
    descends.
Everything hides behind a smile.

In the light that streams through the chinks in the wall you can see my
    face.
There is something important I don't yet understand.
If I plucked even the humblest plant, I would die.

Full of feathers and wings, I launch myself for the gables.
Full of lanterns I will never be lost in the dark.
Full of light and sand, of towering trees,
full of roads and bridges, rivers and waves,
I am filled with the shadow of a leaf on the surface of the water.

How endless my alone-ness!

And a Message on the Way

Someday soon
I will come with a message

and into your bloodstream I will pour light
calling out, "You who haul baskets of slumber and sleepiness, wake up!
    I've brought you an apple, sun-red."

I will come to offer jasmine flowers to the beggar,
to give the leprous woman new earrings,
to the blind man I will say, "How wonderfully sweet and soft the
    garden feels!"

I'll turn into a peddler and roam the twisting market aisles hawking,
"Dew! Get your fresh dew over here!"

A passerby will muse, "It sure is dark out tonight,"
and I will give him a whole constellation completely free of charge.

And the legless girl who begs on the bridge,
around her neck I will string the stars of Ursa Major.

Every mouth will be rinsed free of curses and every wall will evaporate.

I'll tip off the highway robbers,
"A caravan is coming around the bend,
loaded up with a cargo of kindness and smiles."

I'll tear down the clouds
and stitch everyone's eyes to the sun,
and stitch everyone's hearts to love
and sew shadows down into the water's surface,
and sew the branches into the wind's arms.

I'll graft the sleep of newborns to the sound of the summer crickets.

I want to fly kites,
water the flowers,
feed the sweetest alfalfa to the cows and horses.

For the thirsty mule I have a bucket of dew,
I'll fan all the flies away from the tired old donkey.

I've come to plant carnations along the top of each wall,
to sing ghazals at every window,
to give each lonely crow its own white pine,
to say to the snake, "O bless the magnificent frog!"

I will reconcile, understand, walk on.
I will drink light.
I will love.

Bright Existence

Sky, more blue.
Water, even bluer!

I am on the veranda, Rana by the pond in the garden.

She is washing clothes.
Leaves are trickling down.
"What a sad season," my mother said this morning.
I responded, "Life is an apple best eaten unpeeled."

Our neighbor weaves at her window, humming a soft tune.
I am reading the Vedas,
sketching pebbles, birds, clouds—

Full sun.
Starlings flock,
nasturtiums burst into blossom.

And me, cracking open a pomegranate I think to myself,
"If only the seeds of the heart could be so transparent,"

when the juice spurts out and splashes into my eyes,
vermilion tears trickling down.

My mother bursts out laughing
and Rana too.

Water

Let's not stir up any mud in the water.
Downstream, a pigeon may be drinking
or a thrush in the thicket having a bath.
Or someone in the village filling a pitcher.

Let's not stir up any mud in the water.
Maybe it flows past the poplar on its way to soothe some lonely soul,
or the wandering dervish is there, soaking his dry bread crusts.

Someone beautiful approaches the clear reflecting water,
twice as beautiful now.

Sweet, clear stream,
when the townsfolk hear the water lapping at the rocks,
they become happy and their cows produce twice as much milk!

I've never been to that town
but I have no doubt God's footprints track through every flowerbed
and the full moon illuminates their poetry and songs.

No doubt there are only low fences
and every citizen can tell you the difference
between a poppy and a peony.

No doubt blue is bluer there.

And each citizen is attuned to the sound of a bud breaking into blossom.

What an amazing place,
its backroads flooded with the music of the wind.

People who live by rivers understand water.

They do not stir up the mud and neither should we.

Golestaneh

The prairie stretches away,
the mountains reach beyond,
Sweet grass of Golestaneh—

I was searching there—for what?—a dream, a light,
a stone or a smile—

Beyond the poplars
sweet innocence beckons.

I paused by the stand of bamboo to listen as the wind susurrated
    through.
Who was speaking to me?

A lizard slid into the water. I walked on.

Hayfield, cucumber patch, rose bush, oblivion…

At the stream I doffed my sandals to dangle my feet in the water.
How alive I am,
how green like the garden.
So what if sadness creeps down the mountain slope?
Who is that hiding behind the trees?
Only a water buffalo grazing.

High noon.
Shadows know what a summer this is!

Bright patch of sun, sweet spot of shade.
Here's the playground for your childlike urges.

Life is not barren but filled
with kindness, apples, faith
and yes, as long as there are tulips living, we will live too.

In my heart a little flame like the dreams you have
while still half-asleep rousing yourself.

So restless am I that I feel like racing to the end of the desert without
    end,
up to the zenith of the highest mountain
from where it seems there is a voice calling out to me.

Homesickness

The moon hovers over the sleeping village.
On the rooftop terrace there's the smell of the clay bricks of loneliness.
The neighbor's garden is brightly lit,
mine is in darkness.
Moonlight shines down on the plate of sliced cucumber, on a pitcher of
    water.

Frogs sing. Owls hoot.

The mountain looms over us—beyond the maples, beyond the
    juneberry trees.

In the distance, the desert,
its flowers and rocks in darkness,
only its shadow is visible,
like the night-loneliness of a lake or ocean, like an old tune God sings.

It must be close to midnight because there,
just an arm's length out of reach, hangs Ursa Major.

Sky no longer day-blue.

I have to remember to go to Hassan's fruit stand tomorrow
to buy green plums and apricots
and to the slaughterhouse to sketch the goat-carcasses,
sketch the brooms and their reflection in the wet floor...

I must remember to rescue drowning butterflies,
remember not to commit any offense against the laws of the Earth.

I must remember to wash my towel in the stream tomorrow with soapbark.
Remember that I am alone.

The moon hangs in the sky over my loneliness.

The Fish Pass Along a Message

I'd gone to the fountain in the garden
maybe to see my loneliness look back at me,
but the basin was empty.

The fish inside said,

Don't blame the trees—
it was a hot summer afternoon.
Water's bright child lounged here
when the sun-eagle swooped down
and seized him, carrying him off into the sky.

Our scales lost all their brilliance compared with that fiery carnation
    reflected
on the surface. Wind blew across the water and crenellated its petals
and in those folds we lost all our knowledge of air's wily ways.

But that flower was our periscope—
between its ridges and folds, we caught a glimpse
of the garden of Paradise!

Listen, should you see God wandering the paths of the garden
will you make sure to tell Him the fountain has no water…

So the wind goes visiting the sycamore
and I go looking for God.

Address

"Where is the friend's house?" asked the horseman at daybreak.

The sky paused
and the man walking by, who held a branch of light in his mouth,
dropped it to the ground.
Pointing to a white poplar he said,

Just before you reach that tree,
there is an orchard greener than God's dream
where love is bluer than the feathers of Truth's wings.

Walk down the row of trees and come out full from ripening

Turn toward loneliness's flower
Two steps toward the flower, stop

Stay close to the fountain from which flows the various myths of the Earth

You'll be set upon by a calm fear

In the mercurial sincerity of that in-between place you will hear rustling
*   leaves*

There in the high branches of a sycamore
you will see a child
plucking a baby bird from a nest of light

Ask him *where the friend's house is…*

The Oasis of Now

If you are looking for me,
I am beyond nowhere.

Beyond nowhere there is a place
where all messages disperse in the veins of the sky,
bringing news of the blossoming
of all the remote gardens in the far corners of the world.

The ground bears light hoofprints of dainty horses
climbing the poppy-thick hills.

Beyond nowhere there is a place desire opens like an umbrella,
breeze like thirst sinks deep into the leaves.

Bells of rain carol fresh watery tunes
about how lonely humans are here
where the shadows of tree trunks stream into endlessness.

If you are looking for me,
come soft and quietly, lest you crack the glass heart
that cups my loneliness.

Beyond the Seas

I will build a boat
and cast off all lines.
I will sail away from this strange country
where no one awakens the heroes
asleep in the grove of love.

A boat without any fishing nets,
a heart with no interest in pearls.

I'll sail on,
losing heart to neither the endless blue
nor to the sirens
rising from the waves, shaking their hair,
glittering droplets licking the loneliness of the fisherman.

I'll sail on, singing
"Sail on, as far as you can
from the unhappy country where men have no myths,
where women are not full like a cluster of grapes,
where the hall mirrors reflect back only blank space,
where the puddles can't even reflect the street lamp's fire—

"Sail on as far as you can.
Night has sung its tune,
now it is the window's turn."

Still I sail and sing my tuneless tune.

Beyond the seas there is a place
where windows are flung wide open to epiphany
the roofs are thick with pigeons gazing at the streams of knowledge
and every young child holds a gnostic branch in his hand.

The citizens are transfixed by a row of bricks as if it were a flame,
studying it like it was a dream they were fighting to remember.

The soil hears the secret music of your inner feelings.

Overhead phoenixes soar.

Beyond the seas there is a place
where the Sun is as wide as the eyes of the first people awake in the
    morning,

where poets inherit water, wisdom and light.

Beyond the seas there is a place,

you should get started now—
build your boat!

The Friend's Pulsing Shadow

The moon was alive and flooding the sky
as we caught our first glimpse of the city,
our sleeves filled with the night.

We passed an empty ravine,
our ears resounding with the chatter of meadows,
our suitcases bulging with visions of faraway places.

A slight taste of rest in our mouths,
the earth in its rough logic unrolling the road beneath us.
Our shoes, cobbled by prophecy, carry us across the ground
as if we were wind.

Our walking sticks spring eternally on their shoulders.

Each of us in the curve of his own thoughts had a sky tucked away
to rinse blue every corner of her mind.

Each slight gesture of our arms sang of wings fluttering at dawn.

Our pockets full of the chirping canary song of childhood mornings.

We were a whole group of lovers walking past the poorest
      neighborhoods
with their shoreless gifts of pure feeling.

As we leaned over the stream to drink
night evaporated from our faces.

Our ears suddenly caught the whispering voice of a friend...

The Sound of an Encounter

Basket in hand I went to the market square.
Early morning and the fruits are singing in the sun.
Spread out in banks, life dreams of eternal light, the shining perfection
    of rinds.

The orchard's long hours of worry glittered in the shadow of each fruit.
Some unknown thing shone among the quinces.
The pomegranates spread their dark red across the country of the
    pious.

Any thoughts I had about the people around me vanished
before the gleaming ripeness of oranges.

When I returned home my mother asked, "Where is the fruit?"
"How can this one little basket hold infinity?" I asked.
"But I asked you to bring three kilos of good pomegranate!"
"I tried, but the basket could not hold the immensity of even a single
    one."

"And the quinces?" she demanded. "What about our lunch?"

Oh, at noon the image of a quince reflected back from the mirrors
    and stretched from now all the way to end of time…

Night Alone

Listen! A bird chirps in the distance.
The night is warm and soft.
Candlestick flowers, susurrating branches, whispering moon.

Stairs into the house,
lantern hanging near the door,
decadent breeze.

Listen, from the distance the road is yearning for your stride.
Your eyes shouldn't linger in the dark.
Rouse, rouse! Blink awake, put on your shoes, come along
to where the moon's bright feathers brush against your hand,
where Time will sit for a spell while the psalms of the night unreel.
Listen closely to your body and then start to sway gently along…

In that place lives a hermit who whispers to you,
"Seeing eyes drenched with love could teach you a thing or two…"

The Surah of Observation

I swear by Observation!
and the origin of utterance
and the flight of the dove from the mind
that the word is imprisoned.

My lines are clear like the meadow.
I said to them,
"There's a sun knocking on the door that will shed some light
if only you would open it."

And I said to them,
"Rocks are not an ornament for the mountain,
nor is metal jewelry for the axe.
In the palm of the hand of the earth there is an invisible jewel
dazzling all the prophets
with its brilliance.
Go off and find it,
bearing those moments to the meadow of prophethood."

I told them good news of an approaching messenger,
the closeness of that day, its colors growing in number and depth,
the rose's red echo reverberating past the harsh hedges of their
    language.

I said,

"He who sees the garden in the memory of wood
will forever feel the torment of love like a gentle breeze."

"He who makes friends with the birds flying in the sky
will have the calmest sleep on earth."

"He who plucks light from the branches of the tree of Time
can open every window with just a sigh."

We were lounging under a willow tree.
Plucking a leaf from the branch above, I said,
"Open your eyes. What better sign do you seek than this?"

I heard them whispering among themselves,
"He knows the secret of magic!"

On every summit bearing clouds of disbelief on its back
they meet some prophet.

We caressed the wind
so it would rush down and blow off its hat.

Their houses are overflowing with chrysanthemums.

We shut their eyes and did not let them reach for branches of intellect.

Instead we filled their pockets with the ordinary and the everyday.

Then disturbed their slumber and dreams
with the sound of mirrors that face one another, shifting and changing
    and leaving home suddenly for long eternal voyages…

Murmuring Feathers

Snow still unthawed.
Umbrellas like upside-down lotus flowers yet unfurled.
Trees bare of leaf.

Beneath a blanket of snow, damp paper dreams of floating off in the
  wind.
The housefly's dewy gaze.
A frog peeps up over the horizon of understanding.

Our trays are not yet laden with its gossip of samosas and *nowrouz*.
In this weather not a peep from the seedling.
Nor can any tune of feathers beating be heard within the staccato
  stanzas of snow.

I hunger for any sound
but there is still some time until a bird will squawk on March's fevered
  fences.

What can I say then,
I who hunger for just one note in the year's bare songless season?

I better get up,
pick up a brush and dip it in color,
then draw a bright little bird on the canvas of my loneliness.

Bright Leaf of Time

An onslaught of light shook the glass in the door frames.
Morning broke and the sun came up.
We drank tea at the green table of meadow grass.

At nine o'clock the sky clouded over, rain came down.
The fences were wet, my small moments were hidden beneath
    the nasturtiums.
Hidden in the rain, a china doll.

Then the clouds vanished—clear sky—flight of a sparrow.
"Where are all my enemies?"
I thought,
"Their cruelty will melt away before the geraniums."

When I opened the door a piece of sky fell into my glass.
I drank water mixed with sky.
My little moments had their silver dreams.

Under time's invisible roof I opened my book.

Noon. The scent of fresh bread floated from the sunny tablecloth
toward an understanding of the architecture of flowers.
So green is the pasture of understanding!

My hands soak in all the colors of existence.
I was peeling an orange, looking at the city reflected in the mirror.
Where are all my friends? May all their days be orange!

Beyond the window, as much night as you could want.
In my room the soft sound of my fingertip brushing across the sky's
    heights.
From my room the sound of a scale dipping down.

My little moments dreamed all the way to distant stars.
Sleep built on my closed eyes a wide field,
its sands softly humming with the sounds of the footprints
of a friend leading me away…

Sunlight

Sounds of water pouring.
What are they washing in the river of loneliness?
The moment-shirt is clean.

Cold sun. Eighty days before spring.
Snow's echo, a glinting glance, time raining down.
Damp, wet bricks and stones, clean bones of daylight.

What is it we wish for?
The season's mist hovers above the surface of our words.
Mouth: the glass hothouse of thought.

Some voyages dream of you walking through their twisting lanes.
In distant towns the birds congratulate one another
upon your arrival.

Why doesn't anyone understand
the nasturtium was no accident.
Yesterday's river shines in today's fluttering wagtail.

Why doesn't anyone understand
the coldness in the heart that impossible flowers hold?

The Living Word

Beyond the stand of white pines, snow—
Snow, a murder of crows.

The road means strangerhood.
Wind, music, a traveler.
A slow slope up to slumber.
Crest of ivy-covered hills, arrival, yard.

Me, my homesickness, window wet with snow.
I write and: space.
I write and: two walls, a few sparrows foraging.

Someone grieves or weaves, counts or sings.

The meaning of life: the migrating starlings.
What's made you feel this nostalgic?
Look around, happiness abounds: this sun,
the children soon to be born, the dove you saw last week.

Someone died last night.
Bread still bakes.
Rainy snow still drizzles limply down.
The horses drink from the snow-fed trough.

Rain and snow piling down on the shoulders of silence.

Time weighs down on the jasmine's green spine.

From Green to Green

I in this loneliness
dream of a white lamb
come to graze on the grass of my weariness.

I in this darkness
under this rain that soaked the first untried prayer
see my arms reach out to pray.

I in this darkness
open the garden gates
to ancient meadows and the golden lit walls of myth.

I in this darkness
see roots and to the newly growing
sapling of death translate all the rules and regulations of water.

Calling for You

Where are my shoes?
I hear someone calling out, "Sohrab!"

The voice is as familiar to me as air is to the leaf.
My mother is sleeping, my brother Manuchehr and my sister Parvaneh
    too,
probably everyone in town is asleep.

The June night sneaks across the moment like an elegy.
From the hem of my green blanket a cool breeze pilfers the remnants
    of sleep.
My pillow, stuffed with swallows' singing feathers,
has the scent of migration.

Morning will rise
and into the bowl of water the night sky will migrate.

Tonight I will say farewell.

I have spoken to my neighbors through the wide-open window
but don't understand what they are talking about.
None of them glanced down with love to look at the flowers.
None became ecstatic looking at an orchard.
None noticed the magpie.

My heart constricts like a storm cloud
when I see my neighbor Houri
seated beneath the most beautiful and rarest sort of elm
with her nose buried in a textbook of jurisprudence.

Climactic moments:
Once I knew a poet

so absorbed by empty space
the sky laid its eggs in her eyes.

On another night a man asked,
"How long will it take for the grapes to ripen
and swell like the morning sun?"

Oh, I should leave this very minute.

I'll take the suitcase that has enough space for my coat of loneliness
and take off for the mythic forest
where that wordless vastness
keeps calling me.

Again, there it was, did you hear it, someone just called out, "Sohrab!"

Now, where are my shoes…?

To the Friend's Garden

Call me.
Your voice, gentle—
it's the chlorophyll of that strange plant
growing at the very edge of the sincerity of sadness.

In the space of this silent era
I am lonelier than the song echoing through the alley's understanding.

Call me so I can explain to you how deep my loneliness goes,
how it could not predict being waylaid by your fullness.

That's how love goes, I'm told.

There's no one else here.
Let's steal some life for ourselves, divide it between us.
Let's try to learn something from the inner state of stone and rocks.
Let's understand things more quickly.
Look how the minute hand and hour hand of the fountain
pound time to dust on the clock-face surface of the pond.
Come and melt away like a word floating in on my lines of silence.
Come and thaw in my hand like that glittering jewel of love.

Warm me.
Once, on the plains of Kashan, clouds and rain came.
Cold, crouching behind a rock, I was warmed by a hearth of poppies.

In the dark alley I dread the solution to the equation
of matches striking against my doubt and multiplying it.
I dread the century's concrete surface.
Come so I will not fear the cities
whose scorched ground is the nesting ground for tractors and
    bulldozers.

In the age of rising steel open me like a door toward the orchard where
    ripe pears fall.
Lull me to sleep beneath a branch far from the nightly collision of steel
    and stone.

Wake me when the miners come to unearth the ore of dawn.
I will wake with the jasmine flowers held wedged between your fingers.

Then tell me of the bombs that fell while I slumbered, the cheeks made
    wet.

Tell me how many ducks flew in from across the water
when the tanks rolled through crushing the dreams of everyone's
    childhood.

Around whose comforting limb did the canary tie its flaxen string of
    song?

Tell me what sweet cargo was unloaded in the seaports,
which science revealed the music of the smell of gunpowder,
which branch of knowledge billowed forth from the bread
tasted by the mouth of prophets?

Then, like faith warm from tropical sun, I will meet you at the origin
    point of every garden…

Friend: *to Forough Farrokhzad*

"I should be glad of another death." —T. S. Eliot

Wonderful she
A citizen of now
Sister to the horizon
How well she understood the tongues of water and earth

Her voice
reflected the rough sad surface of the real

Her eyes
flickered beneath her closed lids with the pulse of all matter

Her hands
could turn all the pages of the pure air of generosity

Because of her
all manner of kindnesses flocked around us for a morsel

She herself was a mirror reflecting her own singular self
And in the mirror
she reflected all the sensual curves of this moment in time
Like rain she was pregnant with newness and chorusing cadences

Like trees
she opened wide her branches in the sun's radiance

She beckoned to the wind-child
She stitched the water's latch closed with a string of words

And one night she sang for us
the green letter of love so candidly
we caressed the soil
and felt new as we, like flowers, had been watered.

How often we saw her set off
with an empty basket to pluck clusters of good tidings.

But alas
she never had a chance to hear the dove's cogent lectures.
She went all the way past the border of Nothingness.

She never imagined
how lonely we would become
trying to enjoy our fruit
in those briefest of moments
between the slamming shut of doors—

Always

In the evening
a few starlings flew far
from the memory of a white pine.

Exquisite form of the tree emerges,
chaste illumination pouring down across my back.

Speak, evening Betrothed,
and under these branches of mind
return me to my childhood.

Amidst dark forevers
speak to me, my sister of deep colors.

Flood my blood with the leniency of thinking,
read my pulse in the ragged breath of love.

In the land of abstraction
walk to the purity of mythical gardens
at the edge of the possibility that grapes will ripen
to shining sweetness, and speak,
ancient angel of primitive tongues.

Smooth out my sadness in the distant river delta of words.
Project the voice of water as it swirls
through the turbulent boredom of the salt flats.

Spread out on the unruffled grasses of the prairie of perception
        my sweet memory of you, lying back, eyes closed and flickering.

As Far as the Dawn's Heartbeat

Oh, what radiance there is in surfaces that are sacrificed.
Cancer of loneliness, let the surface of Sohrab be a gift for you.

Someone came and stretched my arms
all the way up to the muscles of paradise.

Someone came whose shirt-buttons shone
with the early morning light of new schools of religious thought.

He wove windows with the straw
of ancient chapters and verses.

He was young as the yesterdays of thought.
His voice was suffused with the river's blue virtues.

Someone came, taking away my books,
building a roof overhead out of the architecture of flowers' relationships.

He widened the evening light by adding more windows.
He moved my desk under a roof made out of the rain of spirituality.

Then we sat down to discuss tree-filled moments,
discussed words that dwell best underwater under cloudy skies.

Like the confusion of a sudden appearance of a dove
our moment made a space of light amidst the storm.
It was midnight. Because of the heavy storm of fruit
the idea of a tree contorted itself into a strange new blueprint.

The drenched chain of our dreams was wasted.
Then a hand stirred in the beginnings of a body

and dawn took shape in the elm's wet womb—

مسافر

دم غروب، میان حضور خستهٔ اشیا
نگاه منتظری حجم وقت را میدید.
و روی میز، هیاهوی چند میوهٔ نوبر
به سمت مبهم ادراک مرگ جاری بود.
و بوی باغچه را، باد، روی فرش فراغت
نثار حاشیهٔ صاف زندگی میکرد.
و مثل بادبزن، ذهن، سطح روشن گل را
گرفته بود به دست
و باد میزد خود را.

مسافر از اتوبوس
پیاده ش.
"چه آسمان تمیزی!"
و امتداد خیابان غربت او را برد.

The Traveler

At dusk, amid the exhausted existence of every object and concept in
    the world,
expectant eyes observed the thick air of Time.

On the table, the initial resounding of the season's first fruits
flowed into a most tenuous understanding of death.

Wind carried the scent of the garden upon the soft carpet of leisure
to life's pliant margins.

The flower's bright surface unfolds
and cools us off like a fan held
in the mind's hand.

The traveler
disembarks from the bus exclaiming,
"What a clear sky!"

And road stretching out before him took from him his estrangement.

Evening.

Overheard: the plants rustling an announcement of his arrival.

The traveler entered the garden and sat on a lawn chair.
And spoke:

"I feel sad, how deep and down I feel.
The whole way here I could only think of one thing.
The color of the meadows astounded me.
The road blurred in the field's sorrow.

What valleys!
And the horse—remember? White.

And like the word 'purity' it grazed on the green silence of the fields.

Then the colorful memories of small villages along the way.
Then the tunnel.
I feel sad and spent and like nothing,

Neither these sweet scented moments spinning off the boughs of the
    orange tree
nor the honesty that is wedged between the silence of the night-bloom's
    petals
None of it frees me from the resounding emptiness of every place.

And I believe
I will hear this musical tempo
of sadness forever."

His gaze was focused on the table.

"But what lovely apples!
Life is the distillation of loneliness."

The host asked,
"What do you mean—lovely?"

"Lovely means every form has its own romantic quality.
Love for the apple and love alone can show you truly how sweet one is.
Only love carried me
into the vast sadnesses of many lives
and gave me the chance to become a bird.

And that elixir of sadness?
It tastes like the fountain of youth."

Then darkness fell,
the lights came on,
tea was served.

"Why are you so down?"

"So deep your loneliness!"

"And yours, afflicted by the invisible river of colors."

"And affliction means
'are in love with.'"

"And imagine how lonely the little fish would feel
'afflicted' by the blueness of the infinite sea."

"What delicate and sad thoughts you have!"

"Sadness is the hidden smile of the plants in the garden,
a brief rejection of the idea that all objects and concepts in the world
    are one."

"Aren't the plants lucky to be so singularly obsessed with light,
arms of light stretching around their shoulders?"

"No, unity is impossible.
There's always distance
although the curve of the stream makes a nice pillow
for the sweet slumber of the morning glory.
There is always distance.
One should be 'afflicted'
or else the bewildered murmuring between words
would be wasted. And love is a journey
to a culminating brightness of the solitude of objects.
Love is the echo of distances, the echo of distances drowned
in ambiguity."

"No,
the echo is of distances that are as shiny as silver
tarnished just by hearing the word 'nothing.'
A lover is always alone.

And the lover's hands are in the fragile hands of the clock ticking.
He and the seconds travel to the far side of the day.
He and the seconds sleep on light.
He and the seconds gift the best book in the world to the pond.
And they know full well
no fish has ever managed to untie the thousand-and-one knots of the
    river.
At midnight on the ancient boat of illumination
they set sail on the waters of guidance
and sail on until bewilderment dawns."

"The way you talk
carries one through the garden paths of these stories,
and what strong pensive blood flows
through the veins of your storytelling!"

The yard was brightly lit. Wind picked up.

In the silence of the two men,
the blood of the night flowed.

☙

"A quiet clean room.
What sparseness—a good place to think.
I feel so sad.
I can't sleep yet."

He walked to the window and lay down on the divan.
And thought:

I am still on my journey.

I imagine there is a boat on the oceans of the world
and I, its passenger, for a thousand years

singing the old sailors' lively songs
into the ears of the four seasons.

Still I sail on.

Where is the journey leading me?
Where will the footprints unfinish?
And where will the shoelace be untied
by the soft fingers of tranquility?

Where is the destination where one can spread out a rug,
sit there calmly and listen to someone
washing a dish under the faucet next to me?

In which season will you linger?
And where will the surface of the soul be blanketed
by thick green leaves?

One should drink wine and in the new young shadows one should
    walk.
That is all.

Where is life leading me?
How do I find the hoopoe bird?

And listen, the whole journey is this very word
slammed into the window of slumber.
What was it murmuring in your ears?
Try and remember!

Where is the core of this mysterious tune?

What weighs down on your closed eyes,
what warm sweet weight?

It wasn't a long journey.
The swallows' migration condensed the length of time's book.

And in the dialogue between the wind and the tin roof
I heard the first glimmers of consciousness.

That moment you were looking at the great Jajrud River from summer's
height.

What happened that the starlings harvested your green sleep?

It was the season of harvesting.

A starling alights in the cypress branches,
the book of the season flipped through.

Its first line was: "Life is Eve's one brief minute of colorful negligence."

Should you look:
the wind's mind was racing between the cow and the pasture.

Should you look at the memento of blackberries
collecting on the bark of the season,
amidst the clover the presence of one finch
would heal the scratch on the face of feeling.

Oh look, there is always a scratch on the face of feeling,
always something, like the awareness of a sleeping person
coming from somewhere unseen as gently as the approach of death
putting its arms around us.

And anyhow we drink of the warmth of its touch
like a savory poison.

Do you remember Venice, that quiet canal?

In the quivering quarrel between water and ground
in which Time could be seen through the prism of light,
the rocking gondola shook your mind:
the haze of habit obstructs actual sight.

One should always walk with new breath,
one should take care to breathe deeply to dust off death's golden face.

Where is the Ronus Rock?
I come from the neighborhood of a tree
on whose bark memory's plain hands carved
"For memory I write a line about my sadness."

Pass the wine bottle around.
One should make haste.

I come from an epic journey
and I know by heart the story of
"Sohrab and the Cure."
The journey took me to the garden gate of my childhood.

I stopped to rest when I heard the flapping of wings.

The gate opened and I stumbled to the ground, felled by an onslaught
    of truth.

Once under the sky of the Psalms,
on a journey to the Euphrates, I woke.

There was no lute playing tunefully.

Listening carefully I could hear the sound of weeping
and a couple of lutes were hanging
from the wet boughs of a weeping willow, swinging in the wind.

On the road, several Christian monks
pointed me toward the silent canvas of
"The Prophet Jeremiah."

I recited Ecclesiastes in full voice
while some Lebanese farmers
sitting under an ancient cedar

counted the crop of their citrus orchards
under their breath.

Along the road some blind Iraqi children
were looking at lines from Hammurabi's Code.

On the way I read all the world's newspapers.

The journey was full of flowing,
its surface dull and blackened by industry,
smelling of oil.
The road was full of empty bottles and litter,
gutter of instinct, shadow of fortune
all mixed together.

On the road one could hear coughs
from houses of tuberculosis,
all the whores watching the white streaks of jets in the blue sky.
Children ran after pinwheels.
Street cleaners chanted verses
and the greatest poets were prostrating themselves
before fallen leaves.

The long journey passed through men and steel
toward the hidden essence of life,
the journey joined the damp remembrances of gutters,
the silent flash on a grocery scale,
a voice's familiar tone,
the infinity of a single color.

The journey took me to tropical countries
and under the shade of the great Banyan tree I remember well
a phrase that echoed through the country of my mind:
Be vast, be alone, be humble, be strong.

I arrived from the comradeship of the sun.
Where can I find shade?

I'm still dizzy from the splintering of spring.

The hand of the wind plucks at me, smelling of harvest,
beyond the smoke of the mood of an orange
I lost all sensation
and who knows in the colorful burst
in which niche of the year lies the rock of my repose?

The forest knows nothing
of its own immeasurable measurement.

The leaf still rides
on the wind's first word.

A man still speaks to the water
and in the garden's consciousness there flows
the creek of an argument.

In the tree's orbit an echo
of the pigeon fluttering proves
the vagueness of human deeds.

Listen: a chattering buzz in the air.
I alone am addressed by all the winds of the world.
Its rivers teach me the pure secret of diminishing
and I am the only interpreter of sparrows in all the Ganges Valley.

I have interpreted symbols from the ornate earrings of Tibet
to the bare ears of Varnasi girls walking along Sarnath Road.

Oh Vedic hymn chanted,
put all the weight of newness down on me
for I am still afflicted by the warmth of words
and oh, all the olive trees of Palestine!
Address to me all the riches of your shadow,
to this lone traveler who has hiked around Mount Sinai
and is impatient in the moment of heat at hearing God's direct
    speech.

Yet one day this dialogue will evaporate
and the beauty of butterflies ferrying sensation
will brighten the highways of air.

What rhymes were composed for this operatic sorrow!

Yet still, someone stands under a tree,
still there is a rider behind the castle walls
on whose wet eyes lie the sweet dream of conquest and conversion.

Still the impatient neighing of Mongol horses
coming from the distant alfalfa fields.

Along the Spice Road the merchant of Yazd
is still absorbed by the aroma of Indian spices.

On the banks of the Hamun one still hears:

    —   Evil has contaminated the whole earth!
    —   A thousand years have passed by
    —   No one has heard the sound of bathing
        and no water has reflected any beautiful virgin

Halfway through my journey on the shore of the Yamouna
I saw the reflection of the Taj Mahal in the water.
The endless marble image in that ethereal moment
reminded me of the way measures of life spill into death.

And look, two large wings open
toward the margin of water's soul,
flashing sparkles near the hands
illuminate the darkness of perception.
Only one single hint suffices.

Life is one tender tap
along the the rock of Maghar.

On my journey, the birds in Nishat Garden
rinsed the dust of experience from my eyes
and showed me the vitality of a cypress tree.

I sat by the banks of the River Tal
and in appreciation of the brightness of the moment
I began to whisper the most passionate prayers.

One should cross the river,
accompany the far horizon;
one should sometimes settle in the vein of a single word.

One should cross and eat mulberries from the tip of the branch.
I was walking on the shores of Lyricism.
It was the rich season, the season of blessings.

And under my feet the sands shifted.

A woman heard and came to the window,
looking out, checking the weather.

So young and so delicately
her hands plucked the dew of minutes
from the body of death's feelings.

I paused. The sun of Lyricism rose high in the sky.

I pondered the evaporation of dreams,
counting the number of times that branches of a strange tree
stroke the body of the mind.

We thought we had no margins.
We thought
we were floating amidst legendary debates in the sacred texts.

And that few seconds of negligence is our present existence.

We were at the dangerous beginning of the garden
when that woman caught my eye and said,
"I heard your footsteps.
I thought the wind was blowing through old curtains.
I had heard the sound of you stepping around things."

"Where is the festival of boundaries?"

"Watch the quivering dispersal of my body."

"Which direction will lead me to the greater surface?"

"Feel the distance between me and the brimful glass
with the surface of your thirst."

"When will life be scrutinized as much as a broken glass?
And when will the mystery of the mallow flower dissolve
succulently in the horse's mouth?"

"And once, we heard the sounds of a beautiful gathering of hands
    picking grapes."

"Where was it that we sat on Nothing
and washed our hands and faces in the warm sweetness of an apple?"

"Flashes of improbability emerge from existence itself."

"When will the fear of watching disappear
faster than the route of a bird migrating toward Death?"

"And in the dialogue between people's bodies
how clear was the road of the poplars."

"Which road is it that will lead me to the orchard of all distance?"

Yes, one should cross.

Wind. One should cross.

I am a traveler. O endless winds!

Take me to the vast assembly of leaves.

Take me to the salty infancy of waters.

Fill my sandals with the motion of the beauty of modesty
until the ripening of the grapes.

Fly my moments into the white sky of instinct
all the way up to the circling doves.

Change the moment of me sitting here beside a tree
into pure lost relation.

Into the breathing of my loneliness
send splinters of my intelligence.

Send me flying after the kite of that other day.

Take me to the solitude of life's wan measurements

and show me the presence of soft Nothing.

Notes

Introduction: Quotations from Souroush Dabbagh are translated by Mohammad Jafar Mahallati.

"Water's Footfall":
—Page 13, line 1. Kashan is a city in the province of Isfahan in western central Iran.

—Page 13, lines 9–10. *Qibla* is the direction toward which Muslims pray, no matter where they are on the Earth. The original *qibla* was Al-Aqsa ("the far place" or "the far mosque") in Jerusalem. Later in the ministry of Mohammad the *qibla* was changed to the *ka'aba*, a structure in Mecca said to have been built by Abraham. Its cornerstone is a black stone meteorite built into the wall which pilgrims touch as they circumambulate the building during the *hajj*. In these two lines (a more literal rendering: "My *qibla*, one single rose"), Sepehri is being ironic and serious at once when he says, "I am a Muslim." For more on Sepehri speaking in earnestness and irony simultaneously, see additional notes below.

—Page 13, lines 18–19. *Allahu-Akbar*, meaning "Allah is the Most Magnificent," is called the *takbir-al-ihram*, and is the opening of the call to prayer or *azan* projected over loudspeakers to gather Muslims to the mosque. There are, in fact, two calls to prayer; the second and quieter one closes with "*qad-qamat-as-salaat*" ("Now begins the prayer"); upon its completion the prayer immediately commences.

—Page 14, line 11. Sialk Mound, a major archeological dig site of the ancient Zayandeh Rud civilization, is just outside Kashan.

—Page 16, line 19: *Dhikr* is the repeated mantra Sufis utter as they whirl in devotional ecstasy.

—Page 19, lines 19–21. "From Kashan I am but / there I was not born. / I have no place of origin, no home.": Sepehri was born on the road during a journey his family was taking from Kashan to Teheran. He is flirting, in this phrase, between two meanings, one practical (I have no origin because I was born during a journey) and one more philosophical and mystical. (See note to "Address" below).

—Page 20, line 6. "Heartbeat of the evening that begins Sabbath": In the Muslim system of marking time, a day begins at sunset not midnight. Sepehri's *shab-e-Juma*, literally "Evening of Friday," is, in the Western system, Thursday evening and is the start of Muslim Sabbath.

"Light, Me, Flower, Water": The words in Persian for "solitude" and "loneliness" and those for "solitary" and "lonely" are the same. We've most often chosen, because of the wistful context, to translate it as "loneliness" though in this case neither English option seemed to do.

"Bright Existence": A fairer translation of this title would be "Full Color," referring to the deep-blue sky, but we felt a deep connection between this poem and the early work of American poet Brenda Hillman and so chose this rendering after Hillman's book of the same name, which shares much affinity of style and theme with these poems of Sepehri's.

"Golestaneh": A small village of around 900 people in western Iran, not far from Kashan.

"Address": It isn't made clear by Sepehri whether he means "the friend" as in a literal person or "the Friend," a more religious and Sufi expression of the longed-for Beloved. This coyness about whether one is referring to an ordinary event or elevated meaning is common in Sepehri's work (e.g., "The Friend's Pulsing Shadow," "Bright Leaf of Time," "Calling for You").

"The Oasis of Now": One of Sepehri's most well-known and oft-quoted poems. Its closing lines were used by the people in the 2009 election protests on signs and banners and were stitched onto their clothing. These last three lines are also engraved on Sepehri's tombstone in Mashhad Ardehal, Iran.

"The Surah of Observation": "Surah" means "chapter"; in this case Sepehri is imitating the rhetoric of a Quranic chapter, the first line of which sometimes invokes various abstract concepts and objects (e.g., time, a fig, the morning hour) to be sworn by.

"Murmuring Feathers": Sepehri refers here to *nowrouz*, the Iranian New Year, simply as *eid*. There are several "eids" throughout the year and an Iranian audience would have known to which he was referring. *Nowrouz* falls on the first day of spring. Our "translation" of the Persian *sambosa* into the more common (and therefore unitalicized) English word "samosa" is a moment of cultural hybridity we hope will be not only forgiven but appreciated.

"Bright Leaf of Time": Iranian people commonly spread a sheet or cloth on the floor and sit around it to eat. So the tablecloth isn't, strictly speaking, on a table.

"Sunlight": Eighty days before the first day of spring, the Iranian New Year, a different winter festival is marked. (See "Murmuring Feathers").

"Friend": Forough Farrokhzad (1935–1967) was one of the great contemporary poets of Iran; she is often compared to Akhmatova, Tsvetaeva, Plath, and Sexton. She was killed in a traffic accident. Her work is available in English, particularly in a fine translation by Sholeh Wolpé.

"As Far as the Dawn's Heartbeat": Nearly a decade after this poem invoking the cancer of loneliness, Sohrab would become sick with blood cancer. Though he went to both North America and Europe seeking treatment, he was unable to find it. He returned home and died in a Teheran hospital in 1980.

"The Traveler":
—Page 66, line 13. "Life is the distillation of loneliness": The word we translated as "distillation" is a tricky word used in eschatological discourse to talk about the soul once it has left or transcended the body, but in common use it can connote a state of drunkenness or intoxication. Though not precise, we think "distillation" suggests some of these contexts. Thanks to Charles Peterson for suggesting this translation.
—Page 71, lines 10–11. "I know by heart the story of / 'Sohrab and the Cure.'": Sepehri refers here to a character in the *Shahanameh*, the

ancient poetic epic of Iran. Its episodes, like those of *Le Morte d'Arthur* or the *Iliad* in the West, are known and recited very commonly. One famous story is that of the prince Sohrab who is struck down unknowingly by his long-lost father, who must then search frantically for the potion that will save his son. He may have also been referring to this story when he earlier mentions the "elixir of sadness." Sepehri is obviously also punning on his own metaphorical malady, the "cancer of loneliness," just as through his frequent references to water and rain he is punning on his own name Sohrab, which means "reddening water."

—Page 72, line 26. "The great Banyan tree": Sepehri saw this tree, nearly a half mile in circumference, in the botanical gardens of Kolkata. Throughout "The Traveler" he refers to cities and locales along the route between Kolkata, in India, and Kashan, in Iran.

The Persian text on page 11 is the opening of "Water's Footfall"; on page 27, the poem "The Oasis of Now"; and on page 63, the opening lines of "The Traveler."

Acknowledgments

The poem "Water's Footfall" was published as a chapbook by Omnidawn. Passages from the Introduction to this volume appeared in slightly different contexts in Kazim Ali's essay "The Rose Is My Qibla," which appeared as the chapbook's Afterword. We wish to thank Rusty Morrison and Ken Keegan for their support of Sohrab Sepehri's work and to Cassandra Smith for her beautiful and sensitive design of that edition.

We are grateful to the editors of the following journals who have included poems from this book in their pages:

Excerpts of "Water's Footfall" appeared in "Flowering," a short comic drawn and inked by Craig Thompson, colored by Dave Stewart, and written by Kazim Ali, *CBLDF Liberty Annual 2011*.

"When the Fish Pass Along a Message" appeared in *Faultline*.

"The Oasis of Now" appeared in *Gulf Coast*.

"Beyond the Seas," "The Sound of an Encounter," and "From Green to Green" appeared in *Michigan Quarterly Review*.

"Calling for You" appeared in *The Normal School*.

"When Night Flooded Over," "Light, Me, Flower, Water," "And a Message on the Way," "Bright Existence," "Water," "Golastaneh," and "Homesickness" appeared in *Saginaw*.

We are grateful to Peter Conners and the staff of BOA Editions for their work and support in publishing this book.

A very special thanks to Setareh Sajjadi for typing the original text in Farsi.

Kazim Ali wishes to further thank Asgher Ali for introducing him to the work of Sohrab Sepehri; Marco Wilkinson for first reciting Sepehri to him; Craig Thompson for collaborating with him on the illustrated text "Flowering," incorporating Sepehri's lines; and Sam McWilliams for writing Sepehri onto his body.

About the Author

Sohrab Sepehri (1928–1980) is one of the most widely respected poets of Iran from the twentieth century. A painter and woodworker, his poetry is suffused with lyrical abstractions as well as philosophy influenced by his travels around the world. During his lifetime he published six individual collections of poetry, and a volume of collected work called *Eight Books*, which included two sections of new work.

About the Translators

Kazim Ali is the author of four books of poetry, most recently *Sky Ward* and *Bright Felon: Autobiography and Cities* as well as four books of prose, including *Orange Alert: Essays of Poetry, Art and the Architecture of Silence*. In addition to Sohrab Sepehri, he has also translated works by Marguerite Duras (with Libby Murphy) and Ananda Devi. He is associate professor of Creative Writing and Comparative Literature at Oberlin College, where he teaches courses on poetry, poetics, and translation.

Mohammad Jafar Mahallati is a Presidential Scholar of Religion at Oberlin College where he has taught courses on Islam, the Quran, and the Ethics of Forgiveness and Peacemaking. From 1987–1989 he served as Iran's ambassador to the United Nations and was instrumental in brokering the peace agreement that ended the war between Iran and Iraq. He is currently working on a book project entitled *Friendship in Muslim Cultures: Theory and Practice*.

The Lannan Translations Selection Series

Ljuba Merlina Bortolani, *The Siege*
Olga Orozco, *Engravings Torn from Insomnia*
Gérard Martin, *The Hiddenness of the World*
Fadhil Al-Azzawi, *Miracle Maker*
Sándor Csoóri, *Before and After the Fall: New Poems*
Francisca Aguirre, *Ithaca*
Jean-Michel Maulpoix, *A Matter of Blue*
Willow, Wine, Mirror, Moon: Women's Poems from Tang China
Felipe Benítez Reyes, *Probable Lives*
Ko Un, *Flowers of a Moment*
Paulo Henriques Britto, *The Clean Shirt of It*
Moikom Zeqo, *I Don't Believe in Ghosts*
Adonis (Ali Ahmad Sa'id), *Mihyar of Damascus, His Songs*
Maya Bejerano, *The Hymns of Job and Other Poems*
Novica Tadić, *Dark Things*
Praises & Offenses: Three Women Poets of the Dominican Republic
Ece Temelkuran, *Book of the Edge*
Aleš Šteger, *The Book of Things*
Nikola Madzirov, *Remnants of Another Age*
Carsten René Nielsen, *House Inspections*
Jacek Gutorow, *The Folding Star and Other Poems*
Marosa di Giorgio, *Diadem*
Zeeshan Sahil, *Light and Heavy Things*
Sohrab Sepehri, *The Oasis of Now*

For more on the Lannan Translations Selection Series
visit our website:
www.boaeditions.org